a gift for:

ALice

from:

Olite

Friendship is a sheltering tree.

Samuel Coleridge

Compilation by Rebecca Currington in association with Snapdragongroup℠ Editorial Services, Tulsa, Oklahoma.

Unless otherwise indicated, all Scripture quotations in this book are from the New King James Version (NKJV). Copyright © 1979, 1980, 1982, 1992 Thomas Nelson, Inc. Publisher. Used by permission.

Scripture quotations marked NCV are taken from the New Century Version®. Copyright © 2005 by Thomas Nelson, Inc. Used by permission. All rights reserved.

Scripture quotations marked THE MESSAGE are taken from *The Message: The Bible in Contemporary Language*. Copyright © by Eugene H. Peterson 1993, 1994, 1995, 1996, 2000, 2001, 2002. Used by permission of NavPress Publishing Group.

Scripture quotations marked NRSV are taken from the New Revised Standard Version of the Bible. Copyright © 1989 by the Division of Christian Education of the National Council of the Churches of Christ in the United States of America and are used by permission. All rights reserved.

Scripture quotations marked CEV are taken from the Contemporary English Version. Copyright © 1991, 1992, 1995 by the American Bible Society. Used by permission.

Scripture quotations marked NLV are taken from the Holy Bible, New Life Version. Copyright © 1969-2003. Christian Literature International, P. O. Box 777, Canby, OR 97013. Used by permission.

J Countryman® is a trademark of Thomas Nelson Inc.

Editorial Director: Todd Hafer
Art Director: Kevin Swanson
Illustrator: Chun Wang
Designer: Michelle Nicolier
Production Artist: Dan Horton

ISBN: 978-1-59530-149-9

Printed and bound in the United States of America

BOK3087

friendship
is a blessing

Inspirational Reflections on Friendship

friendship
is a blessing

Inspirational Reflections on Friendship

introduction

Friendship and women go together like coffee and creamer, pizza and pepperoni, mascara and eyeliner, long, dangly earrings and a plush cashmere turtleneck. It's natural. Doesn't it seem that, as soon as we can speak, we go in search of people we can share secrets and stories with?

That longing for soul support is a God thing—an inner motivation to seek out those who will be there for us in the hard times and challenge us to be our authentic selves at all times.

As you pirouette through the pages of this book, we hope you will find yourself moved to tears and bursting with laughter, unable to stifle a hearty "Oh yeah, Baby!" You may even find yourself yearning for a new friend. If so, put on your "friend-shopping" shoes and go out in search of that someone. She's probably out there looking for you right now!

A friend may well
be reckoned the
masterpiece of nature.

Ralph Waldo Emerson

Wang

what is a friend?

It's better to have a partner than go it alone.

Share the work, share the wealth.

And if one falls down, the other helps....

Ecclesiastes 4:9–10 THE MESSAGE

the essence of friendship

To have a good friend is one of the highest delights of life; to be a good friend is one of the noblest— and most difficult—challenges. Friendship depends not upon fancy, imagination, or sentiment, but upon character. There are none so poor that they are not rich if they have a friend; there are none so rich that they are not poor without a friend.

Friendship is a word made to cover many kindly, impermanent relationships, but real friendship is abiding. Like charity, it is patient and kind. Like love, it does not promote itself, but pursues the even tenor of its way, unafraid of a bad report, loyal in adversity, the shining jewel of happy days.

G. T. Hewitt

Women don't just have friends.
We have soulmates…
and that is powerful compensation
for life's other hardships.

Alarie Tennille

Trust in the power
of other people
who can help you
to accept and love yourself.

Ann Kaiser Stearns

The greatest blessing
is a pleasant friend.

Horace

The glory of friendship
is not the outstretched hand,
nor the kindly smile,
nor the joy of companionship;
it is the spiritual inspiration
that comes to one when
he discovers that someone else
believes in him and is willing
to trust him.

Ralph Waldo Emerson

the abc's of friendship

A Friend:

A · Accepts you as you are.

B · Believes in you no matter what.

C · Calls you just to say "hi."

D · Doesn't give up on you.

E · Envisions the whole of you
(even the unfinished parts).

F · Forgives your mistakes and shortcomings.

G · Gives of herself to you unconditionally.

H · Helps you without being asked.

I · Invites you to come over.

J · Just wants to "be" with you.

K · Keeps you close to her heart.

L · Loves you for who you are.

M · Makes a difference in your life.

N · Never judges you.

O · Offers you her support.

P · Picks you up when you're down.

Q · Quiets your fears.

R · Raises your spirits with her encouraging words.

S · Says nice things about you.

T · Tells you the truth when you need to hear it.

U · Understands you.

V · Values you.

W · Walks beside you through the hard times.

X · "Ex"-plains those things you don't understand.

Y · Yells as loud as it takes to make you listen.

Z · Zaps you back to reality.

a friend is:

A push when you've stopped.

A word when you're lonely.

A guide when you're searching.

A smile when you're sad.

A song when you're glad.

A friend is someone

who understands your past,

believes in your future, and accepts

you today, just the way you are.

*

One of the secrets of life
is to keep your friends
within hugging distance.

Anonymous

True friends have no
solitary joy or sorrow.

William Channing

A true friend prods you
to personal growth,
stretches you to your full potential.
And most amazing of all,
celebrates your successes
as if they were his own.

Richard Exley

I do not wish to treat friendships
daintily, but with roughest courage.
When they are real, they are not
glass threads or frostwork,
but the solidest thing we know.

Ralph Waldo Emerson

A true friend unbosoms freely,
advises justly, assists readily,
adventures boldly, takes all patiently,
defends courageously, and
continues a friend unchangeably.

William Penn

friendship is . . .

F • Forgiving

R • Refreshing

I • Inspiring

E • Encouraging

N • Nurturing

D • Dependable

S • Sincere

H • Honest

I • Inviting

P • Patient

The best kind of friend
is the kind you
can sit on a porch and swing with,
never say a word,
and then walk away
feeling like it was the best
conversation you've ever had.

✳

Hold a true friend
with both hands.

Nigerian proverb

Two friends, two bodies
with one soul inspired.

Homer

A true friend is the person
in whose light
we shine the brightest.

Keely Chace

My friends are my estate.

Emily Dickinson

a friend is loving

A friend loves at all times.

Proverbs 17:17

I love you not only for what you are, but for what I am when I am with you. I love you not only for what you have made of yourself, but for what you are making of me. I love you for the part of me that you bring out.

Elizabeth Barrett Browning

I love you for what you are, but I love you yet more for what you are going to be. I love you not so much for your realities as for your ideals. I pray for your desires that they may be great, rather than for your satisfactions, which may be so hazardously little…you are going forward toward something great. I am on the way with you and therefore I love you.

Carl Sandburg

Friendship is Love without his wings.

Lord Byron

So what is the key to friendship? What one quality or characteristic do you look for? If you could pick only one trait to have in a friend, which one would you choose? Honesty? Dependability? Sense of Humor? Loyalty? While all these qualities are wonderful and valuable to any relationship, there is still another characteristic that is necessary to sustain a friendship through anything and everything—and that's love.

Love has so many qualities all wrapped up in one amazing package; it's almost impossible to define. But if anything can make a friendship lasting and worthwhile, it's love. In fact, a friendship without love is really a mere acquaintance. Even the most casual friendships are made up of at least a small amount of love. And the friendships we cherish the most always begin and end with love.

Melody Carlson

Take my love, for love is everlasting.
And remember the truth that once
was spoken: to love another person
is to see the face of God.

From *Les Miserables*

Life is to be fortified
by many friendships; to love
and to be loved is the
greatest happiness of existence.

Sydney Smith

Love is an act of will: listening to someone when you are bored, keeping that perfectly couched comeback to yourself, letting a friend win the argument over something unimportant, biting your tongue instead of reminding them of your triumphs, hearing a friend out one more time on the same old saw (and hoping she will return the favor). Love is not waiting to feel good before plunging into these and other unselfish acts, but rather love is the decision to treat your friends a certain way even when you feel like Ms. or Mrs. Grump.

Leslie Williams

The impulse of love that leads us to the doorway of a friend is the voice of God within, and we need not be afraid to follow it.

Agnes Sanford

The supreme happiness of life is the conviction of being loved for yourself, or more correctly, being loved in spite of yourself.

Victor Hugo

What brings joy to the heart is not so much the friend's gift as the friend's love.

Saint Aelred

"I accept you as you are."

"I believe you are valuable."

"I care when you hurt."

"I desire only what is best for you."

"I erase all offenses."

We could call that the ABC's of love. And I don't know of anybody who would turn his back on such magnetic, encouraging statements.[1]

Charles Swindoll

Rare as true love is
true friendship is still rarer.

François De La Rochefoucauld

Don't walk in front of me,
I may not follow.
Don't walk behind me,
I may not lead.
Walk beside me and be my friend.

Albert Camus

We have been friends together
in sunshine and in shade.

Caroline Norton

So many of my
favorite stories begin,
"One time, my best friend and I…"

Tina Neidlein

The truth is, friendship is
to me every bit as sacred
and eternal as marriage.

Katherine Mansfield

It's the friends you can call up
at 4 a.m. that matter.

Marlene Dietrich

Love…
puts up with anything…
always looks for the best.

1 Corinthians 13:6–7 THE MESSAGE

a friendship prayer

Dear Lord,

Thank you for the love you've placed in my life through the friends you've given me. They bring me warmth when the days are cold, music when I'm overwhelmed by silence, joy when sadness dawns above and below me. May I be a loving friend to each one of them as well. Fill me anew with your love that I may pass it along.

Amen.

a friend is kind

Love each other as brothers

and sisters and honor

others more than you do yourself.

Romans 12:10 CEV

Our journeys through life
are brightened by the acts
of kindness and caring
of the friends
we make along the way.

✳

premeditated kindness

While I appreciate the notion behind the book title *Random Acts of Kindness,* I have to question it a bit. For I wonder: How is it possible for kindness to be done randomly? Isn't an act of kindness an intentional act that requires premeditation or at least a commitment to thoughtfulness? How can that be random?

Perhaps what the author intended to suggest was that kindness can be done here and there, throughout one's day in a random sort of way. And, I must agree, that's a wonderful idea—one that Jesus taught, in fact, when He spoke of being a good Samaritan, or giving in secret, or blessing your enemies.

The beauty comes when we make these kind acts appear to be random. But I think it takes a little planning and preparation.

Melody Carlson

A little thought and a little kindness
are often worth more than
a great deal of money.

John Ruskin

Be kind. Remember that everyone
you meet is fighting a hard battle.

Harry Thompson

Friends cherish each other's hopes.
They are kind
to each other's dreams.

Henry David Thoreau

The sun makes ice melt; kindness
causes misunderstanding, mistrust,
and hostility to evaporate.

Albert Schweitzer

Kind words are the music of the
world. They have a power which
seems to be beyond natural causes,
as though they were some angel's
sons who had lost their way
and come to earth.

Frederick Faber

True friends are those
who really know you
but love you anyway.

Edna Buchanan

The best exercise
for strengthening the heart
is reaching down
and lifting people up.

Ernest Blevins

Be the living expression
of God's kindness: kindness
in your face, kindness in your eyes,
kindness in your smile, kindness
in your warm greeting.

Mother Teresa

Kind words can be short
and easy to speak, but their echoes
are truly endless.

Mother Teresa

Kind words are never wasted.
Like scattered seeds, they spring up
in unexpected places.

E. M. Bounds

It is not so much our friends'
help that helps us
as the confident knowledge
that they will help us.

Epicurus

Somebody

Somebody did a golden deed;
Somebody proved a friend in need;
Somebody sang a beautiful song;
Somebody smiles the whole day long;
Somebody thought, 'Tis sweet to live.
Somebody said, "I'm glad to give";
Somebody fought a valiant fight;
Somebody lived to shield the right;
Was that "somebody" you?

*

make a moment

Two women move, each along her own course of life,
then…a brief glance and shoulders brush. Somehow,
in the flash of that moment, a kindred understanding transpires. It may be the comforting touch of
an emergency-room nurse as your frightened child
is mended. Or the knowing smile of a classy older
woman in the checkout line as you discreetly attempt
to discipline your unruly four-year-old. Perhaps it's a
businesswoman's concerned eyes that meet yours
across a tense conference room. Somehow you know
she understands. She thinks like you do. It can happen
in all sorts of places and at various stages of life, yet
somehow you know intuitively that this is a woman
who understands what you're going through—a
woman you can relate to. How precious are these
moments! Like priceless jewels, they encourage our

hearts when we need it most for it's in those difficult situations that we most need—and appreciate—small acts of kindness. Afterwards, we bless that sweet "sister" who took the time to show us kindness. We remember her for days, even years, to come.

Consider what little effort it takes to reach out to a sister in need: Offer to hold a fussy baby while the flustered mother fumbles in her purse for her checkbook. Smile encouragement at a young woman who's obviously down on her luck. Gently squeeze an elderly woman's hand. They may only be small tokens of love, yet they mean so much. What a wonderful gift to share passing moments of sisterhood with other women along life's way. It's hard to tell who is most blessed—the one who receives, or the one who gives.

Melody Carlson

If you've ever planned a surprise party or a secret act of kindness, you know how much fun all the preparation and build-up of suspense can be. Then standing on the sidelines and watching the whole thing unfold is absolutely incredible! When you put kind thoughts, energy, and creativity into giving an anonymous gift or doing a secret act of kindness—it's nothing short of thrilling.

Melody Carlson

Jesus said: "When you do something for someone else, don't call attention to yourself….When you help someone out, don't think about how it looks. Just do it—quietly and unobtrusively. That is the way your God, who conceived you in love, working behind the scenes, helps you out."

Matthew 6:2–4 THE MESSAGE

Little kindnesses
will broaden your heart.

Zadik

We secure our friends
not by accepting favors
but by doing them.

Thucydides

a circle of friendship

Drop a stone into the water——
In a moment it is gone.
But there are a hundred ripples
Circling on and on and on.
Say a word of cheer and splendor——
In a moment it is gone,
But there are a hundred ripples
Circling on and on.

a prayer of thanks

Dear Lord,

I don't know what would have become of me
were it not for the kindness of the friends you've
placed in my life. They have lifted my head and
given me a cool drink of water when I was
exhausted and thirsty. They have opened their
homes to me as well as their hearts. Help me to
bless them with kindness in return.

Amen.

a friend is loyal

Some friends play at friendship, but a true friend
sticks closer than one's nearest kin.

Proverbs 18:24 NRSV

the treasure of a true friend

Loyalty is one of those qualities that shines brightest in the hard times. Unless something goes wrong, you might never appreciate its value. But when life is hard, a true friend will always make you glad that you invited her into your life. How will you know if your friend is loyal? It could be that she speaks up when she hears someone putting you down. Or maybe when it seems you are the least popular person on the planet, she's still there, at your side, still saying she will be your friend forever and proving it. If you are fortunate enough to find even one loyal friend—hold her close and never let her go!

Rebecca Currington

giving thanks for friends

"A friend will joyfully sing with you when you are on the mountaintop, and silently walk beside you through the valley."

"A friend is the one who comes in when the whole world has gone out."

Even as David thanked God for Jonathan and praised him in well-remembered lines, so have we abundant reasons to thank God today for friends and to resolve to keep these friendships in constant repair.

Edgar DeWitt Jones

A friend who holds your hand
and says the wrong thing is made
of dearer stuff than the
one who stays away.

Barbara Kingsolver

One loyal friend is worth
ten thousand relatives.

Euripides

A true friend is someone
who is there for you when
he'd rather be anywhere else.

Len Wein

Friends always have something
to say to each other,
and sometimes they don't
even need words.

Sarah Mueller

A friend doesn't go on a diet
because you are fat. A friend
never defends a husband
who gets his wife an electric skillet
for her birthday. A friend
will tell you she saw your
old boyfriend and he's a priest.

Erma Bombeck

The friends of my friend
are my friends.

French proverb

True friendship is loyalty
to a friend in trouble.

Ralph Brewer

friends in tough times

Dear Lord,

I thank you for the friends who have stood by me during this difficult time. To be honest, I didn't expect them to stay, but they did—to the very end. They believed in me and prayed for me. They dared to associate with me even when my integrity was questioned. And when the truth was revealed, they acted as if it was no surprise. They never doubted, and their confidence in me never wavered. Help me to be just that kind of friend—a loyal friend—to those you've placed in my life.

Amen.

a friend is trustworthy

One who is trustworthy in spirit

keeps a confidence.

Proverbs 11:13 nrsv

The essence
of a perfect friendship
is that each friend
reveals himself
utterly to the other,
flings aside his reserves,
and shows himself
for what he truly is.

Robert H. Benson

To throw away an
honest friend is, as it were,
to throw your life away.

Sophocles

building trust, piece by piece

Nothing makes us feel quite so vulnerable as placing our heart and soul in the hands of another. Yet this is the level of trust and honesty we long for with our dearest friends—and hope they find with us. For to have a friend is to be a friend; it's impossible to separate one from the other.

And how is this kind of trust achieved? How do we know if our friends are truly trustworthy? How do we know if we are?

Trust is knowing that you can be transparently honest with your friend. It's the assurance that your deepest secrets, your strongest desires, your biggest dreams, even your worst mistakes are safe in the hands of another. It's believing that your friend will not betray your confidence. It's knowing she has your best interests at heart. But a foundation of trust is built slowly, one piece at a time. For only as we become convinced that one portion of our life is safe with a friend can we hand over another. In other words, we don't usually dump everything about ourselves onto a brand-new friend. We take it slowly and carefully— wisely revealing only what seems appropriate—until our confidence in our friend increases along with her confidence in us. After a while, we know without a doubt that the foundation of trust is strong and firm. We don't even question it anymore. Instead, we find that a truly good friend can even discern when we're not being totally honest—with her or with ourselves.

Melody Carlson

Few delights can equal the mere presence
of one whom we trust utterly.

George MacDonald.

The highest sign of friendship is that of giving another
the privilege of sharing your inner thought. It is a
personal gift in which there is self-commitment.

Paul Tournier

Oh, the inexpressible comfort of feeling safe
with a person; having neither to weigh thoughts
nor measure words, but to pour them all out,
just as they are, chaff and grain together,
knowing that a faithful hand will take and sift them,
keep what is worth keeping, and then,
with the breath of kindness, blow the rest away.

George Eliot

A friend will tell you the truth. Even when it hurts. Even when the truth threatens your friendship. Because she knows that there is no real friendship without truth.

Sarah Mueller

Everybody needs some friends around who will say, "You are wrong!" And that includes me. I really value the friendship of people who'll just tell it to me like it is.

Billy Graham

There's a special kind
of freedom friends enjoy.
Freedom to share
innermost thoughts, to ask a favor,
to show their true feelings.
The freedom to
simply be themselves.

✳

Where there is great love,
there are always miracles.

Willa Cather

a prayer of healing

Dear Lord,

There were times when I trusted no one.
I assumed that everyone would be untrue.
But you've taught me to trust again, and you've
placed wonderful friends in my life who are
trustworthy. Thank you for this wonderful gift.
Help me to be a trustworthy friend as well—
trusting as I am trusted.

Amen.

a friend is forgiving

One who forgives an affront fosters friendship.

Proverbs 17:9 nrsv

Even the very best friend isn't perfect. Every friendship has its share of ups and downs, disappointments and discouragements. But the true test of friendship is whether it endures the hard times as well as the happy times.

When you are truly best friends—when you have a friendship worth preserving—you learn how to voice your feelings with each other. You discuss how and when you've been hurt. You even cry together. Then you forgive, seal your friendship with a hug, and continue on good terms with each other.

That's how best friendships are maintained over the years. Each little offense is dealt with and forgiven (and forgotten). The focus remains on the strengths of the relationship—love, understanding, acceptance, and loyalty. When you take time to work through differences and misunderstandings, the friendship grows stronger and sweeter.

Melody Carlson

We pardon to the degree
that we love.

François de La Rochefoucauld

Every person should keep a
fair-sized cemetery lot in which
to bury the faults of friends.

Henry Ward Beecher (paraphrased)

Friendships aren't perfect,
and yet they are very precious.

Letty Cottin Pogrebin

The essence of true friendship
is to make allowances
for another's little lapses.

David Storey

A friend should bear
his friend's infirmities.

William Shakespeare

Forgiveness is a funny thing.
It warms the heart
and cools the sting.

William Ward

To err is human,
to forgive divine.

Alexander Pope

Humanity is never so beautiful
as when praying for forgiveness
or else forgiving another.

Jean Paul Richter

dear friend,

We've been through so much together,

The laughter, the blahs, and the tears.

My life would be boring without you.

What would I have done all those years?

I don't want to take you for granted,

Or ever forget to forgive,

For I hope that our friendship will last

Just as long as we both get to live.

And one day when I go to heaven,

(I hope when I'm very old.)

I'll say: "Thank you, Lord, for my friend.

She's been worth her weight in pure gold!"

Melody Carlson

when hearts unite

The way that friends' hearts unite is a true mystery. Even friends themselves cannot fully explain, or even understand, it. But it's here. And it's real.

We are loyal—fiercely so. And yet, we don't hesitate to point out each other's flaws or blind spots— sometimes bluntly. But oh, how we are able to for- give—totally and completely! Perhaps it's because we are so alike, so connected. It's as if we're simply forgiving ourselves.

Let's promise each other, dear friend, that we'll always be ready to listen, able to love, and quick to forgive. Let's reaffirm our commitment to friendship and make sure we never allow any offense, whether big or small, to come between us or divide us. For there's no one on earth quite like a friend. And even one day lost to resentment or bitterness is one day too many.

*

God planned for
our lives to connect.
Let's make sure
we keep it that way.

Melody Carlson

A friend will never sugarcoat
a bad situation, but she'll also never
pronounce it hopeless—
because no situation is hopeless
when you have a friend
by your side.

Sarah Mueller

"Who seeks a faultless friend
remains friendless."

Turkish proverb

thanks for a forgiving heart

Dear Lord,

Thank you for one of the greatest gifts
ever given—the forgiving heart of a friend.
It is a thing of beauty, fashioned after your own,
great act of forgiveness. It graces my life like a
sweet fragrance, reminding me to handle
the flower of friendship tenderly, lovingly, careful
not to bruise its bloom.

Amen.

a friend is honest

One who gives an honest answer

gives a kiss on the lips.

Proverbs 24:26 nrsv

A truly good friend cares about you so much she's willing to lay your friendship on the line. She's willing to tell you the truth, even when it hurts—or isn't what you want to hear. She'll wrap the truth in a thick layer of love, but she won't hesitate to be honest and candid when she knows that's what you need to hear.

A true friend will speak up if she feels you're dating the wrong guy or being too hard on your husband or letting a job stress you out. She sees your blind-spots—those areas of life you prefer to overlook or deny. A true friend will speak out, even if she risks offending you because she cares about you. And she knows that in time you'll come to your senses, forgive her, and even thank her!

Melody Carlson

A truly good friend
will openly correct you.
You can trust a friend
who corrects you,
but kisses from an enemy
are nothing but lies.

Proverbs 27:5–6 CEV

there's nothing like a good girlfriend

When the chips are down, there's nothing like a good girlfriend. A friend is someone who accepts you—warts, wrinkles, weight, and all—unconditionally. She will listen to you cry or complain and do her best to look out for your best interests. She supports you through thick and thin, but because there is mutual respect, she will not allow you to wallow in self-pity or manipulate her. She will encourage you to be your best self and allow you the freedom to make your own choices.

All women are born with the need to communicate at a deeper level with their mothers, grandmothers, sisters, daughters, aunts, cousins, and other significant females in their lives. Wholesome friendships among women promote sound mental and emotional health. Friends remind us we are part of something greater than ourselves, a larger world, and the right friends keep us on track.

Barbara Jenkins

The best mirror is an old friend.

George Herbert

You know you've found a friend
when her opinion matters more
than what the billions of other
people in the world think.

Sarah Mueller

The better friends you are,
the straighter you can talk.

Saint Francis Xavier

A friend is one who incessantly pays us the compliment of expecting from us all the virtues, and who can appreciate them in us.

Henry David Thoreau

To speak painful truth through loving words—that is friendship.

Henry Ward Beech

be yourself

We are the most appealing to our friends, and the happiest within, when we are completely ourselves. But it is a constant struggle because, as Scripture teaches, the world is always trying to press us into its mold. The mold of the world is the mold of the synthetic, the mold of the artificial, the mold of the celluloid—the "Plastic Person." The world cries, "You've got to be young and you've got to be tan. You've got to be thin and you've got to be rich. You've got to be great." But Scripture says, "You don't have to be any of those things. You simply have to be yourself—at any age—as God made you, available to him so that he can work in and through you to bring about his kingdom and glory." Now relax. Trust him and be yourself!

Luci Swindoll

From acquaintances we conceal
our real selves. To our friends
we reveal our weaknesses.

George Basil Hume

A true friend can never have
a hidden motive for being a friend.
He can have no hidden agenda.
A friend is simply a friend,
for the sake of friendship.

James Houston

Friends, if we be honest
with ourselves, we shall be honest
with each other.

George MacDonald

Honesty has a beautiful
and refreshing simplicity about it.
No ulterior motives. No hidden
meanings. An absence of hypocrisy,
duplicity, political games, and
verbal superficiality. As honesty and
real integrity characterize our lives,
there will be no need
to manipulate others.

Charles Swindoll

an "honest" prayer

Dear Lord,

Honesty is something one deeply hopes for in a
friend. So precious is it, and rare, that to have one
honest friend in a lifetime is more than could be
expected. When one is found, what amazing joy—
to know that there is one person in all the world
who can be depended on to speak the truth
regardless of the circumstances. Such a friend is a
treasure, Lord, and a blessing beyond measure.

Amen.

wang

a friend encourages

Encourage each other every day.

Hebrews 3:13 ncv

the power of affirmation

Women can understand and affirm each other on a feminine level, which can strengthen and encourage us. Think of the strength Jesus' mother, Mary, and her cousin, Elizabeth, brought to each other during their pregnancies and the births of Jesus and John the Baptist. God gave each of them a task that neither of them could fully comprehend. He gave them wonderful, supportive husbands, but he also gave them each other. They must have giggled with delight behind closed doors as they shared each other's joy and marveled over God choosing them to take part in the most wonderful miracle of all time. They must have also encouraged each other's faith. . . .

That's what we women do for each other, and that is why we need each other.

Gayle Haggard

When you talk,
do not say harmful things
but say what people need—
words that will help others
become stronger.

Ephesians 4:29 NCV

comfort and encourage

Job's friends pelted him with unrelenting words. Like torrential rains on parched soil, their words gouged deep gullies. Job attempted to escape like a tired swimmer, only to be crushed with a fresh wave of words. His comforters rapped him with anger, guilt, idle chatter, ignorance, and faulty conclusions. And he remained crushed instead of wrapped in comfort.

Do your words rain down comfort? Love chooses to cover instead of condemn. Job's choice confronts us daily. Some people provoke us to exchange blow for blow, gossip for gossip, curse for curse, rebuke for rebuke. To speak as Job's "comforters" spoke requires no wisdom or strength from God. That kind of speech comes naturally. But if we choose to use our words to encourage and comfort, we will need supernatural strength. God is ready when you are.

Jan Carlberg

Every time we
encourage others,
we give them
a transfusion of courage.

Chuck Swindoll

You have the ability with your words to make people stronger. Your words are to their souls what vitamins are to their bodies.

✳

Do not withhold encouragement from the discouraged. Do not keep affirmation from the beaten down! Speak words that make people stronger. Believe in them as God has believed in you.

Max Lucado

There are deep sorrows and killing
cares in life, but the encouragement
and love of friends were given us to
make all difficulties bearable.

John Oliver Hobbes

Sometimes our light goes out
but is nurtured into flame
by another human being.
Each of us owes deepest thanks
to those who have
rekindled this light.

Albert Schweitzer

A genuine friend encourages
and challenges us to live
out our best thoughts,
honor our purest motives,
and achieve our most
significant dreams.

Dan Reiland

The most precious gift that one
person can bestow on another
is gentle encouragement.

Phillip Keller

a friend is a blessing

Dear Lord,

Encouragement is in short supply these days.
We all long for someone who will offer a kind word,
support us as we pursue our dreams,
and help us to look up when the day is long
and night even longer. I thank you for
the encouragers in my life. Return to them the rich
blessing they provide for others.

Amen.

Wang

a friend is fun-loving

A merry heart does good, like medicine.

Proverbs 17:22

enjoying one another

A poet once described friends as "the sunshine of life." I myself have found that the day is certainly much brighter when I'm sharing it with my friends. Enjoying fellowship is one of life's sweetest blessings and joys. What would we do without people and the many shadings of companionship and camaraderie?

We need friends in our lives, friends with whom we discuss "deep" issues and confide our secrets, fears, or sorrows—and with whom we can laugh, play, and even cry. The best times in life are made a thousand times better when shared with a dear friend.

Luci Swindoll

A real friend is not so much
someone you feel free to be
serious with as someone you feel
free to be silly with

Sydney J. Harris

friendship keeps us balanced

Life today is difficult. Problems challenge us, and we worry about our children's futures. It's easy to fall into the trap of taking ourselves too seriously, of worrying about success, jobs, acceptance, parenting, illnesses, and so on. It's easy to lose our ability to laugh. It's easy to forget the simple ways of purely enjoying one another. Friendship keeps us balanced in a difficult world, renews our perspective, and enables us to recapture joy.

Susan Yates

easy entertainment

Do you remember how easily you could be entertained as a child simply with a friend by your side? Just sitting on the front porch discussing who was the cutest boy in the sixth grade could occupy you for hours, as could walking barefoot together on a hot summer's afternoon while quietly slurping a vanilla ice-cream cone. Somehow, doing nothing with your best friend was an event.

And remember years later when you dropped in on your best friend and shared a cup of stale morning coffee, laughing together as you helped her fold a week's worth of laundry? Somehow, by the time you left, the world seemed a happier place. That's the beauty of a great friendship—it makes even the mundane parts of life colorful.

Melody Carlson

Give me your laugh. Whether it's
mischievous, tender, loud, or quiet,
simply give me a laugh from your
heart. Your laughter
brings me never-ending joy.

Helmut Walch

Laughter is not at all a bad
beginning for a friendship,
and it is far the best ending for one.

Oscar Wilde

Happiness isn't the easiest thing
to find, but one place
you're guaranteed to find it
is in a friend's smile.

Allison Poler

That is the best—
to laugh with someone because
you both think
the same things are funny.

Gloria Vanderbilt

celebrating life

How much tastier is a cup of delicious gourmet coffee or tea when shared with someone special—someone who savors the taste as much as you do! How much more pleasureable is an incredible art exhibit when shared with a friend who appreciates Van Gogh as much as you do! Why is it that these experiences are enhanced and magnified when just the right person is there to delight in them with us?

Perhaps because life suddenly becomes a celebration—an occasion to warm the heart. If you think about it, how often do we celebrate in isolation?

When something is worth commemorating, we want others to share it with us. And that's just one of the great pleasures that come with a special friend. She helps us celebrate life more fully—she enriches our experience, adding sparkles and laughter and love!

*

Everyone needs friends.
When you're with them, you can
be totally lost, yet feel right at home.
You can be heartbroken, yet find
yourself giggling uncontrollably.
You can be doing something that
should be completely boring
and realize that you're having
the time of your life.

Sarah Mueller

Friendship is a present
you give yourself.

Robert Louis Stevenson

Jesus surrounded himself with close friends here on earth. And while his purpose was to reveal himself and his ultimate plan for salvation, one can't help but notice that he also enjoyed a good time with his friends. In fact, he often described himself as the bridegroom, saying how it was time to celebrate—to eat, drink, and enjoy his presence.

Good friends are like that. They bring an air of festivity and celebration into an otherwise ordinary day. Life without dear friends is like watching *The Sound of Music* in black and white with the volume turned off—flat and gray and silent.

So celebrate the divine gift of friendship. Enjoy the color and dimension it brings into your day—and give it back in full return! Life is for living, and friends are one of the most enjoyable ingredients.

Melody Carlson

Real friends have
a great time
doing absolutely
nothing together.

✳

a gift from god's heart

Dear Lord,

Who could ask for more than a friend
with whom I may relax and enjoy myself—
someone eager to see the humor
in a situation and turn my heart to laughter?
I feel that such a friend is a gift
straight from your heart.
Bless us as we play and laugh
and enjoy the life you've given us.

Amen.

celebrating old friends

Do not forsake your own friend

or your father's friend.

Proverbs 27:10

Make new friends,

but keep the old;

Those are silver,

these are gold.

Joseph Parry

When I needed encouragement, you gave me a pep talk.

When I required help, you rolled up your sleeves.

When I wanted to talk, you picked up the phone.

When I needed a hug, you opened your arms.

When I had to vent, you lent me your ears.

When I needed a nudge, you gave me an elbow.

When I required correction, you did it ever so gently.

When all I could do was cry, you cried right along with me.

And when I needed to pray, you opened your heart.

Melody Carlson

There is no friend
like an old friend
who has shared
our morning days,
no greeting like his welcome,
no homage like his praise.

Oliver Wendell Holmes

My coat and I live
comfortably together.
It has assumed all my wrinkles,
does not hurt me anywhere,
has molded itself on my
deformities, and is complacent
to all my movements,
and I only feel its presence
because it keeps me warm.
Old coats and old friends
are the same thing.

Victor Hugo

a priceless treasure

A best friend is a priceless treasure. And like a rare jewel, her value appreciates over time. In other words, she's worth hanging on to. Friendships like this don't come along every day, and that's why they're worth all the time and energy you can invest in them. In fact, the more you invest in them, the more valuable they become.

But what happens when hundreds or even thousands of miles separate you from a friend you hold dear? You'll need to take special measures to keep the doors of communication open. Like a priceless jewel, you'll need to give the friendship a little buffing and polishing from time to time, so it doesn't lose its splendor and grow dull.

How do you maintain a long-distance friendship? Through letters, telephone calls, e-mails, cards, gifts, and a visit from time to time. You can also pray for each other no matter how many miles separate you.

＊

The best way to keep your friends is not to give them away.

Wilson Mizner

However you choose to do it,
keep in touch! For just as a rare
jewel is most precious to the owner
who understands its value,
so is a treasured friend.
Don't let the distance between you
be anything other than miles!

Melody Carlson

friendship grows sweeter

The really best of friends—the women who are closer than sisters—are those friends who've been through a lot together. They've enjoyed the good times, and comforted each other during the tough times. They're the ones you telephone to share some wonderful news; they're the ones you run to when your heart is breaking. You know they'll stick by you no matter what. They'll always be there.

They're also the ones you share the ordinary, everyday things of life with. You know they won't yawn with boredom when you tell them about Katie's first tooth or that Jamie is struggling in English or that your perennials just aren't blooming well this year.

*

This kind of friend will laugh
at your jokes—or tell you they're not
funny without hurting your feelings.
She's the one you confide in when
you're worried about
your marriage, your finances,
your health, your faith.
You can be completely candid
and honest, for you know she won't
judge you. When she gives
you advice, you know it's worth
listening to, for she has
your best interests at heart.

Melody Carlson

It is one of the blessings
of old friends
that you can afford
to be stupid with them.

Ralph Waldo Emerson

thank heaven for old friends

Dear Lord,

You have given me such good friends. Many are new, but a few have been in my life for a very long time. I don't really remember what I did before they were there. Who held my hand when I was frightened? Who told me a funny story when I was sad? Who stood up for me when I was being disrespected and disapproved? Old friends are the best. They are proven, tried, and true. Thank you, Lord, for old friends.

Amen.

Friends are the sunshine of life.

John Hay

It takes a long time
to grow an old friend.

John Leonard

I cannot even imagine where
I would be today were it not for that
handful of friends who have given
me a heart full of joy. Let's face it,
friends make life a lot more fun.

Charles Swindol'

acknowledgements

The creators of *Friendship Is a Blessing* thank the following authors and publishers for allowing us to use material from previously published works:

Melody Carlson, *Women Are Sisters at Heart,* (Nashville: J. Countryman, a division of Thomas Nelson, Inc., 2000), fourteen selections used by permission.

Leslie Williams, "Seduction of the Lesser Gods," (Nashville: W Publishing, 1997), used by permission.

Charles Swindoll, *Dropping Your Guard,* (Nashville: W. Publishing Group, 1983), two selections used by permission.

Max Lucado, *A Love Worth Giving, (Nashville: W Publishing 2002),* two selections used by permission.

Rebecca Currington, *"The Treasure of a Friend,"* an original essay, used by permission.

Barbara Jenkins, *Wit and Wisdom for Women,* (Nashville: Thomas Nelson, 1996), used by permission.

Gayle Haggard, *A Life Embraced,* (Colorado Springs: WaterBrook Press, 2004), used by permission.

Jan Carlberg, *The Hungry Heart,* (Brentwood, Tenn.: Wolgemuth & Hyatt, 1991), used by permission.

Luci Swindoll, *You Bring the Confetti, God Brings the Joy,* (Nashville: Word, 1986, 1997), used by permission.

Susan Alexander Yates, *A House Full of Friends,* (Colorado Springs: Focus on the Family, 1995), © Susan Alexander Yates, used by permission.

Sarah Mueller, *The Best of Friends* (Kansas City: Hallmark Licensing, Inc., 2006), four selections used by permission.

we'd love to hear from you
if you have enjoyed this book

Please send your comments to:
Book Feedback Mail Drop 215
2501 McGee, Kansas City, MO 64108
or email us at
booknotes@hallmark.com